Revved Up and Ready to Go!

An Easy-to-Sing, Easy-to-Stage Kid's Musical about the Race of Your Life

Created by Heidi Petak

Performance time: 22 minutes

Lillenas.com

Contents

Cast

Announcer 1 – Male, enthusiastic, good enunciation, announces the beginning and end of the race. Wears a button-up shirt, tie, and headphones.

Announcer 2 – Female, enthusiastic, good enunciation, announces the beginning and end of the race. Wears a nice shirt and headphones.

Julie – Little sister of JIMMY, precocious but with a positive attitude. Wears casual clothing.

Jimmy – Big brother of JULIE, has less of a positive attitude than his sister, must be able to snap his fingers. Wears casual clothing.

Harold – Husband of HENRIETTA, stubborn, older man. Wears adult clothing and glasses.

Henrietta – Wife of HAROLD, confused, older woman. Wears adult clothing and glasses.

Mike – Authoritative, persuasive. Wears a trench coat and sunglasses.

Click – Brother of TICK, radio personality, expert on cars. Wears an auto mechanic jumpsuit.

Tick – Sister of CLICK, radio personality, expert on cars. Wears an auto mechanic jumpsuit.

Ashley – Frustrated caller to CLICK and TICK'S radio show, sensitive, spiritual and emotional. Wears casual clothing.

Non-speaking roles: RACER 1 and RACER 2 *(these two kids race for a candy bar in Scene 1)* and SHELLI (optional) when ASHLEY pantomimes calling her.

SCENE 1

*(*ANNOUNCER 1 *and* ANNOUNCER 2 *sit next to each other behind a table. They each speak enthusiastically into microphones on table stands.)*

ANNOUNCER 1 & ANNOUNCER 2: Ladies and Gentlemen! Welcome to "The Race of Your Life!"

ANNOUNCER 2: I'm *(name of girl announcer).*

ANNOUNCER 1: And I'm *(name of boy announcer).*

ANNOUNCER 2: We are coming to you live from *(church name).*

ANNOUNCER 1: The race we're getting ready for today is the toughest event in the world of racing.

ANNOUNCER 2: Tougher than the Daytona 500.

ANNOUNCER 1: Tougher than the Indy 500.

ANNOUNCER 2: And tougher than the race between two kids for one candy bar.

*(*ANNOUNCER 1*stands on his chair and holds up a candy bar. Two kids from the choir jump off the risers and race to get it.* RACER 1 *jumps but cannot reach it. While he continues jumping,* RACER 2 *uses a "grabber" with a long handle to "grab" the candy bar.)*

ANNOUNCER 2: *(Name of* RACER 1*)* is first off the risers. But *(name of* RACER 2*)* is close on his heels! Wait! It looks like *(name of* RACER 2*)* came prepared to win! Well, would you look at that! *(Name of* RACER 2*)* wins the candy bar hands down.

*(*ANNOUNCER 1 *sits.* RACER 1 *and* RACER 2 *return to their places.)*

ANNOUNCER 1 *(to* RACER 2*)*: Congratulations *(name of* RACER 2*)*! *(To audience)* So if you want to be ready

ANNOUNCER 2: If you want to win,

ANNOUNCER 1: Then you need to get your heart ready for "The Race of Your Life!"

ANNOUNCER 1 & ANNOUNCER 2: Ladies and Gentlemen, start your engines!

Rev It Up!

Words and Music by
CARTER ROBERTSON
and BARNY ROBERTSON
Arr. by Barny Robertson

CD: 1
CD: 41

Driving ♩ = ca. 200

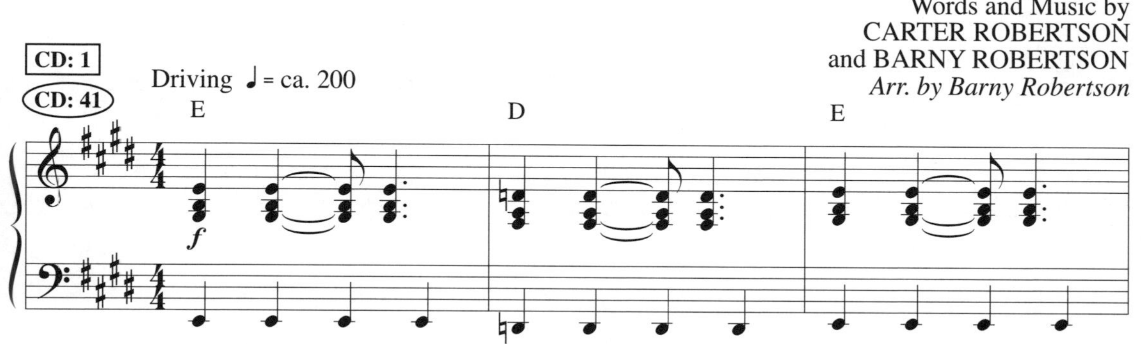

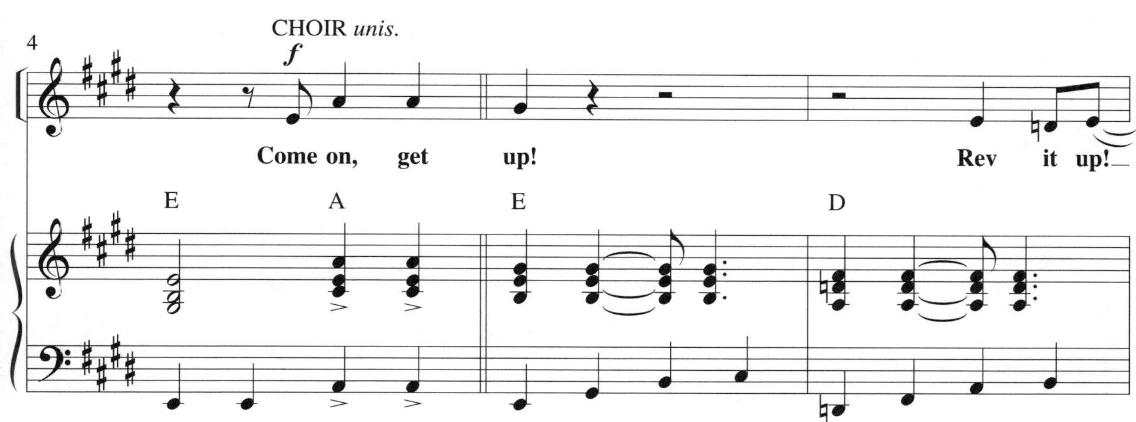

10
up!) Rev it up! (Rev it up!) Come on, get
D E A
13
up! (Come on, get up!) Rev it up! (Rev it up!)
E D E
CD: 2 1st time
CD: 5 2nd time
16
Come on, get up! (Come on, get up!) Rev it up!
E A E D
CD: 42 1st time
CD: 45 2nd time
Optional cued harmony notes both times
19
(Rev it up!) Rev it
E A G

22
up, let's go! Whoop! Whoop! Let's roll!
G
E
25
Rev it up! Rev up the love in your soul! Let's
G
A
28
go! Rev it up, let's go!
E
G
31
Whoop! Whoop! Let's roll! Rev it
E
G

CD: 3 1st time
CD: 6 2nd time
CD: 43 1st time
CD: 46 2nd time
34
up! Rev up the love in your soul! Let's go! I've got
G A C
37
full throt - tle strength, And God's love makes me stand
E A E
40
strong. And if I see you start to sink I'm gon - na
A E A
43
reach out to you; Lift you up, and help you come a - long.
F♯ B +

CD: 4 1st time
CD: 7 2nd time
46
GROUP 1
(Group 2 add cued notes 2nd time)
GROUP 1
Come on, get up! (Come on, get up!) Rev it up!
B+
8va
gliss.
E
D
CD: 44 1st time
CD: 47 2nd time
49
Group 2
GROUP 1
(to pg. 5, meas. 9)
Group 2
(Rev it up!) Come on, get up! (Come on, get
E
A
E
52
up!) Rev it up! (Rev it up!) Come on, get
D
E
A
55
up! (Come on, get up!) Rev it up!
E
D

57
(Rev it up!)
Come on, get
E
A
59
CHOIR Opt. div.
up! (Come on, get up!)
Rev up the love in your soul! Let's
E
D
E
62
go! Rev up the love in your soul! Let's go! Rev up the
E
A7
C
65
love in your soul! Let's go! Rev up the love in your soul! Let's
A7
E
A7

SCENE 2

*(*JIMMY *and* JULIE *stand at microphones)*

JULIE: So if you want to be ready for "The Race of Your Life", you first need to rev up the love in your heart!

JIMMY: But that's not always easy.

JULIE: Like . . . when?

JIMMY *(pulls a glitter-painted racecar out from behind his back)*: Like when a certain little sister paints my favorite racecar with glitter.

JULIE: I just thought it needed a little pizzazz.

JIMMY: But when I see glitter like this *(referring to the car)*, it takes away the love in my heart like that *(snaps his fingers)*.

JULIE: Then I know what you need.

JIMMY: More pizzazz?

JULIE: No, you need to ask Jesus for a custom-built heart!

Custom-built Heart

Words and Music by
CARTER ROBERTSON
and BARNY ROBERTSON
Arr. by Barny Robertson

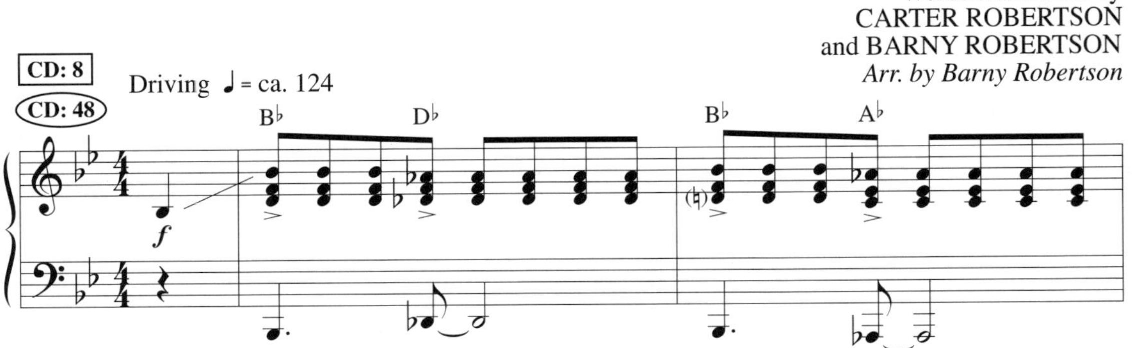

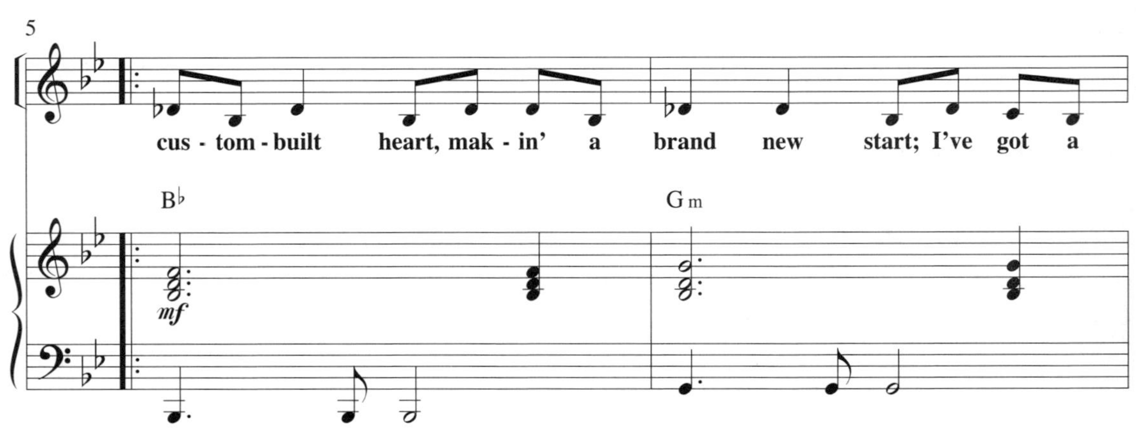

7
revved up and read - y soul. My love's full
B♭ E♭ B♭
9
throt - tle strength, it goes to an - y length; A
B♭ F Gm
11
high per - form - ance mind, watch me grow– In - to a
E♭ F B♭
13
Opt. harmony
"ped - al to the met - al" kind of neigh - bor. I'll
E♭ D♭

15
love 'em, like Je - sus loves me; His love is
E♭ F B♭ E♭/B♭ B♭
CD: 9 1st time
CD: 11 2nd time
CD: 49 1st time
CD: 51 2nd time
17
strong, His love is true, it will not wav - er, I wan - na
E♭ D♭
19
love with my words and deeds. Love
Cm7 F Gm7 G♯°7 F7/A
21
God! And be read - y! Stand
B♭ D♭ B♭ A♭

23
strong! And be smart! Love God and
B♭ D♭ E♭ F
25
oth - ers! A strong and stead - y, A -
B♭ D♭ B♭ A♭
CD: 12 2nd time
CD: 52 2nd time
27
simp - ly ask Je - sus for a cus - tom - built heart. Yeah! Yeah!
F Gm7 G♯°7 F7/A
CD: 10
CD: 50
29
1
Tune it up! A - Yeah! Yeah!
B♭ D♭ B♭ A♭

31
mf (to pg. 12, meas. 5)
Tune it up!
I've got a
B♭
D♭
E♭
F
33
2
cus - tom - built heart. Love
God! And be
G♯°7
F 7
A
B♭
D♭
35
read - y! Stand
strong! And be
B♭
A♭
B♭
D♭
37
smart! Love God and
oth - ers! A strong and
E♭
F
B♭
D♭

39
steady - y,
A - simp - ly ask Je - sus for a
B♭
A♭
F
G m7
41
cus - tom - built heart. Yeah! Yeah!
Tune it up!
G♯°7
F7/A
B♭
D♭
43
A - Yeah! Yeah!
Tune it up!
B♭
A♭
B♭
D♭
45
Yeah! Yeah!
Tune it up!
E♭
F
B♭
D♭

SCENE 3

*(*HAROLD *and* HENRIETTA, *dressed as older adults, sit on two adjacent chairs as if they are in a car.* MIKE *sits in a chair behind them as if he is in the backseat. He is dressed like a spy in a trench coat and sunglasses.)*

HENRIETTA *(looking at a map)*: Harold! Do you think we should take I-640 or Highway 110?

HAROLD *(mimes steering)*: I don't know, Henrietta. I'm not the one with the map.

HENRIETTA: Well, all I know is that all these lines are very confusing. *(Lowers map)* Why don't we stop and ask for directions?

HAROLD: Oh no, no, no, no, Henrietta. I refuse to put my self-respect on the line by stopping to ask for directions.

*(*MIKE *rises behind them.* HAROLD *continues driving and* HENRIETTA *continues looking at her map as if* MIKE *is not present.* MIKE *puts a hand on the backs of each of their chairs and uses an Announcer-type voice.)*

MIKE: Poor Harold and Henrietta. They don't know which way to go. When you don't know which way to go, call 1-800-N-O-W-P-R-A-Y, that's 1-800-NOW-PRAY and ask Jesus for directions. Because Jesus doesn't just know the way; He is the way.

Jesus Is the Way

Words and Music by
PAM ANDREWS
Arranged by John DeVries

10
The Way,
He is the Life,
He is the Truth, He is the Life.
Dm7
Gm9
C

13
the Way,
Je - sus is the Way.
Our Fath - er, Sav - ior, Mas - ter, Helps us
F
Dm7
Gm9

16
in dis - as - ter.
Je - sus is the One and on - ly,
C
B♭
Am
Dm7

CD: 14 1st time
CD: 54 1st time
CD: 16 2nd time
CD: 56 2nd time
1st time: CHOIR
2nd time: SOLO
19
Jesus is the Way.
1. It's a-
2. Je-sus
Gm7 C F B♭ F
22
maz-ing what can hap-pen, when we're
says for us to fol-low and do
B♭/C F2/A
24
fol-low-ing the Lord. We can make a dif-
what His Word com-mands. Tell the world a-bout
B♭/C F2/A Gm7
27
-f'rence, He can o-pen an-y door. And with
Him, Je-sus Christ the great I AM. He will
F2/A E♭ C

30
Him we can move moun - tains, we can
lead you thro' the val - leys, lead you
B♭/C
F2/A
32
sail the o - cean wide. He
to the moun - tain - tops. When
B♭/C
F2/A
34
brought His pow - er to the earth when
Je - sus came He brought the world a
Gm7
F2/A
36
on the cross He died.
love that nev - er stops.
1
CD: 15
CD: 55
(to pg. 19, meas. 5)
E♭
Csus/D
C
B♭2
C

39
2
CD: 17
CD: 57
CHOIR unis.
Je - sus is the Way.
Csus/D
C
C2
D
D/F♯
G
SOLO
42
The Way,
He brings us joy and laugh - ter, Life for -
Em7
Am9
44
The on - ly Way,
ev - er af - ter.
Je - sus is the Way.
D
G

46
the Way.
He is the Truth, He is the Life.
Em7
Am9
48
He is the Life,
Je - sus is the Way.
D
G
50
the Way,
Our Fath - er, Sav - ior, Mas - ter, Helps us
Em7
Am9

52
in dis - as - ter. Je - sus is the One
D
C
54
My Je - sus.
and on - ly, Je - sus is the Way.
Bm Em7 Am7 D G
57
(Stage whisper)
Je - sus is the Way. The Way!
Am7 D G D7sus G

SCENE 4

*(*CLICK & TICK *sit at a table speaking into the table mics used in the first scene)*

CLICK: Welcome to Car Chat.

TICK: The radio show where my brother and I fix your worst life problems . . . I mean . . . car problems.

CLICK: You might be going the right way, but if car trouble slows you down, you ain't goin' no where, no how.

TICK: Let's go to the phones. Hello! You're on the air!

*(*ASHLEY *steps up to a microphone on a stand with her cell phone up to her ear.)*

ASHLEY: Hi. This is Ashley.

CLICK & TICK *(together)*: Hi Ashley!

TICK: So tell us about your life . . . I mean . . . your car.

ASHLEY: My car won't go above 30 miles an hour. It's like it has no power!

CLICK: No power? Hmm. Sounds like a transmission lock-up torque converter to me.

ASHLEY: A what?

TICK: What my brother means is….there must be someone in your life you haven't forgiven.

ASHLEY: Oh no! You must mean Shelli. But you don't know how bad she hurt my feelings!

CLICK: I'm sure she did. But if you don't learn to forgive your friend and forget it, you won't have the power you need to finish . . .

CLICK & TICK: . . ."The Race of Your Life!"

ASHLEY: Really?

CLICK & TICK: Really!

*(*ASHLEY *hangs up with Car Chat hosts as song begins. Then during the song,* ASHLEY *prays and mimes calling Shelli on the phone to forgive her. During the last line of the song, she hangs up her phone.)*

Forgive and Forget

Words and Music by
PAM ANDREWS
Arranged by John DeVries

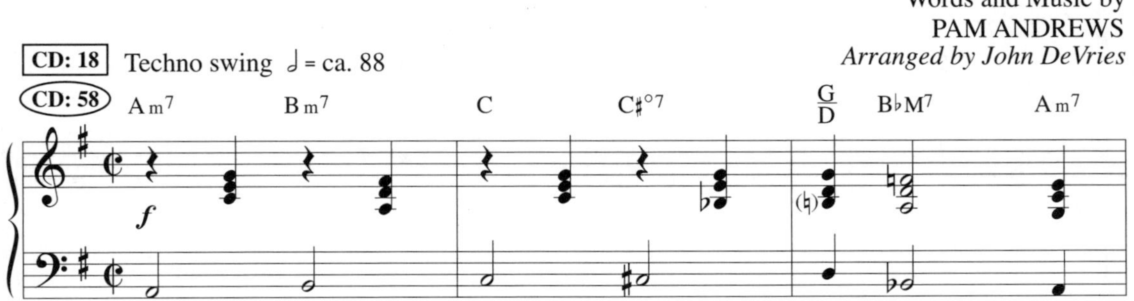

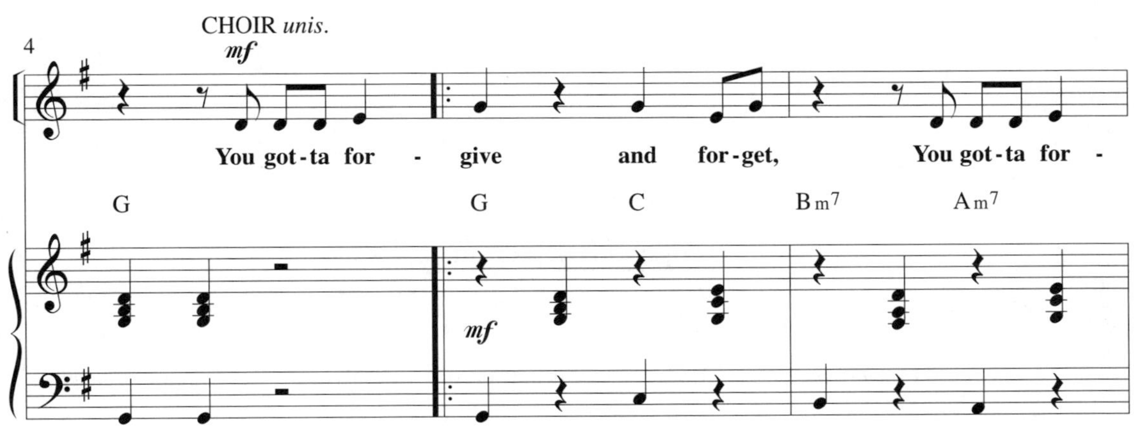

10
heav'n - ly joy and Je - sus' hap - pi-ness. So when some -
E7#9
A9 Bm7 C6 A7/C# D7 D
13
one has done you wrong, Just give it to Je - sus in a song.
G B7 C
CD: 19 1st time
CD: 59 1st time
CD: 21 2nd time
CD: 61 2nd time
16
In or-der to live, you got-ta for - give and for-get.
A7 Am7 D7sus
19
1st time: CHOIR
2nd time: SOLO 1
1. Some - one has hurt you thro' and thro'.
2. So please be - lieve me, this is true;
G F7 F#7 G C9

22
You think your heart might break in two.
For-giv - ing is some - thing you must do.
C9
G

24
You think you'll nev - er, ev - er
You will feel bet - ter fol - low -
G
C9

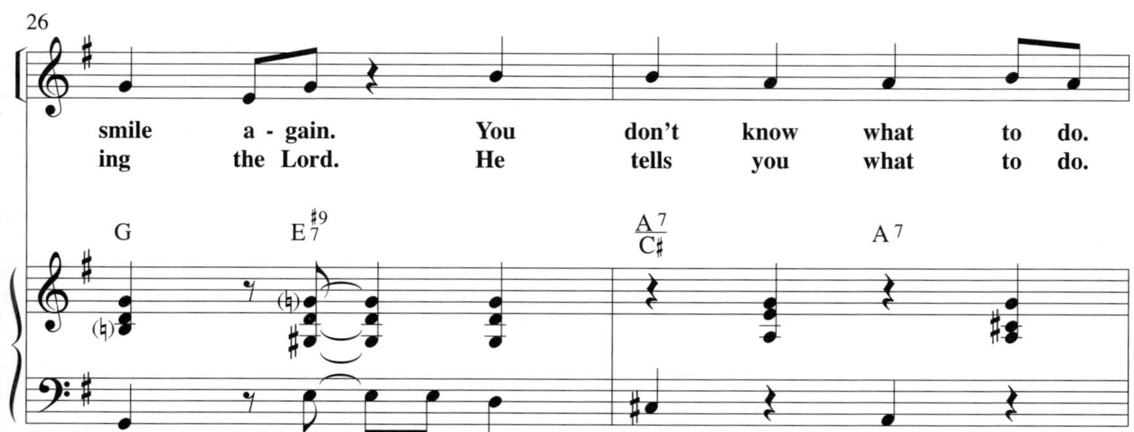
26
smile a - gain. You don't know what to do.
ing the Lord. He tells you what to do.
G
E7#9
A7/C#
A7

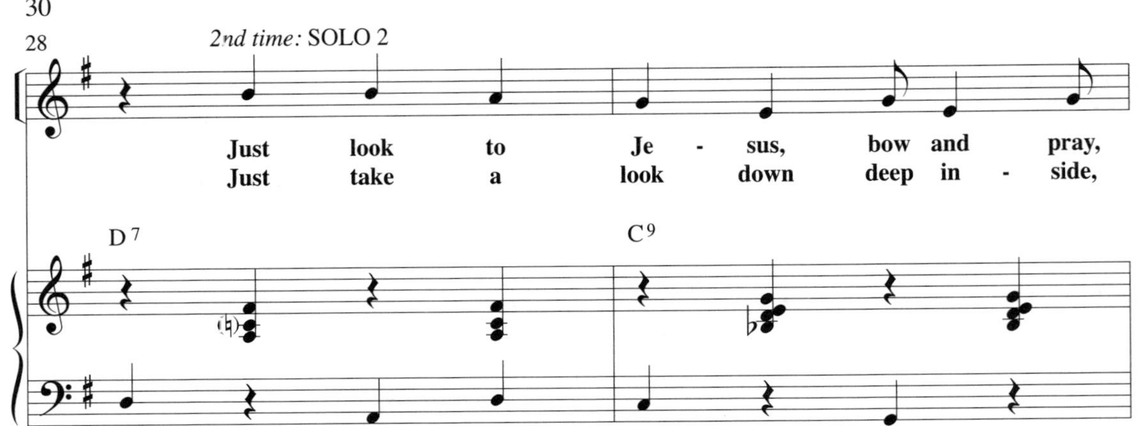
28
2nd time: SOLO 2
Just look to Je - sus, bow and pray,
Just take a look down deep in - side,
D7
C9

30
And He will take your pain a - way.
the Lord will glad - ly be your guide.
C9
G

CD: 20 1st time
CD: 60 1st time
CD: 22 2nd time
CD: 62 2nd time
32
In or - der to live, you got - ta for -
In or - der to live, you got - ta for -
G
D9sus

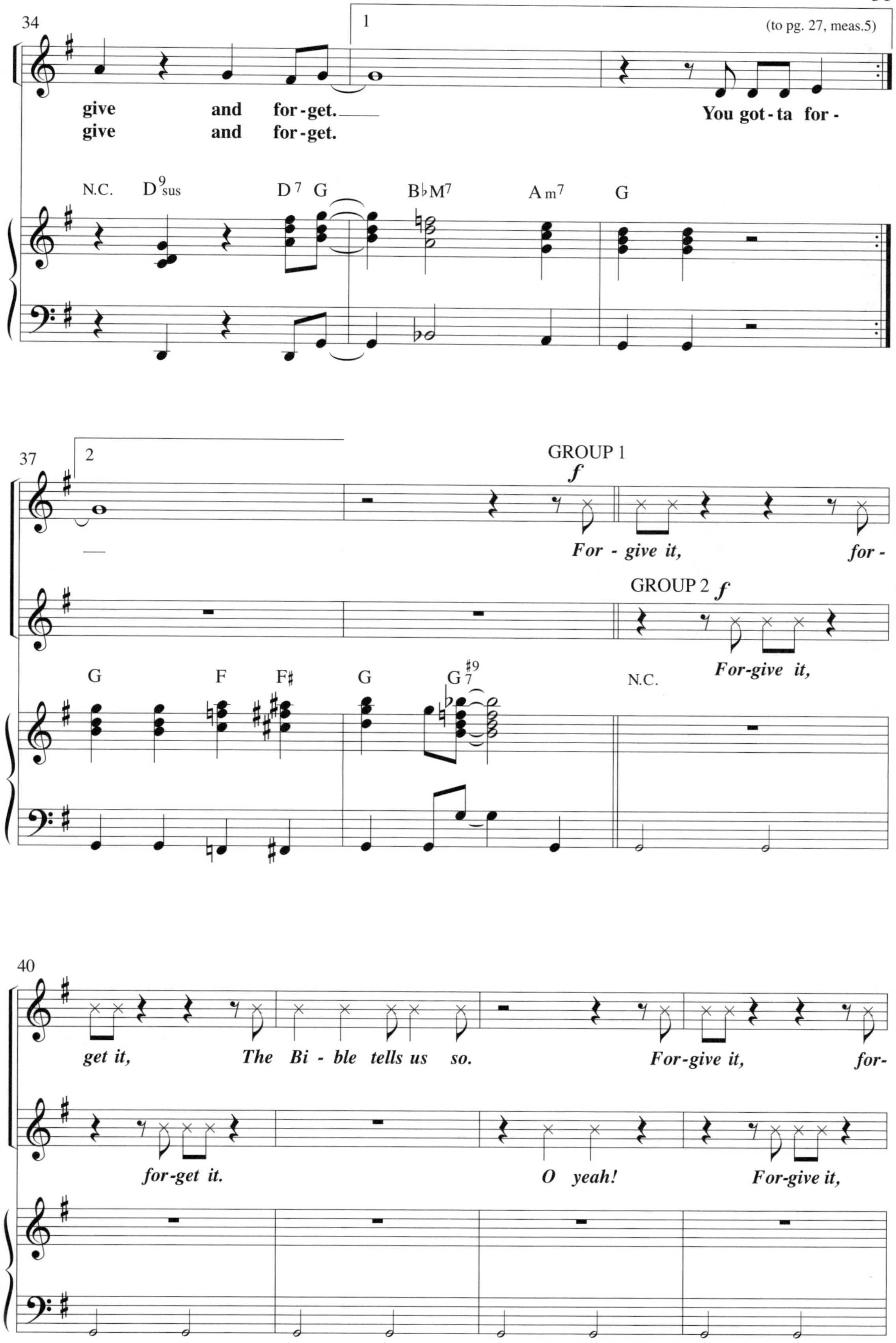

34

1

(to pg. 27, meas.5)

give and for-get. You got-ta for-

give and for-get.

N.C. D9sus D7 G B♭M7 Am7 G

37

2

GROUP 1

f

For - give it, for -

GROUP 2 *f*

For-give it,

G F F♯ G G7♯9 N.C.

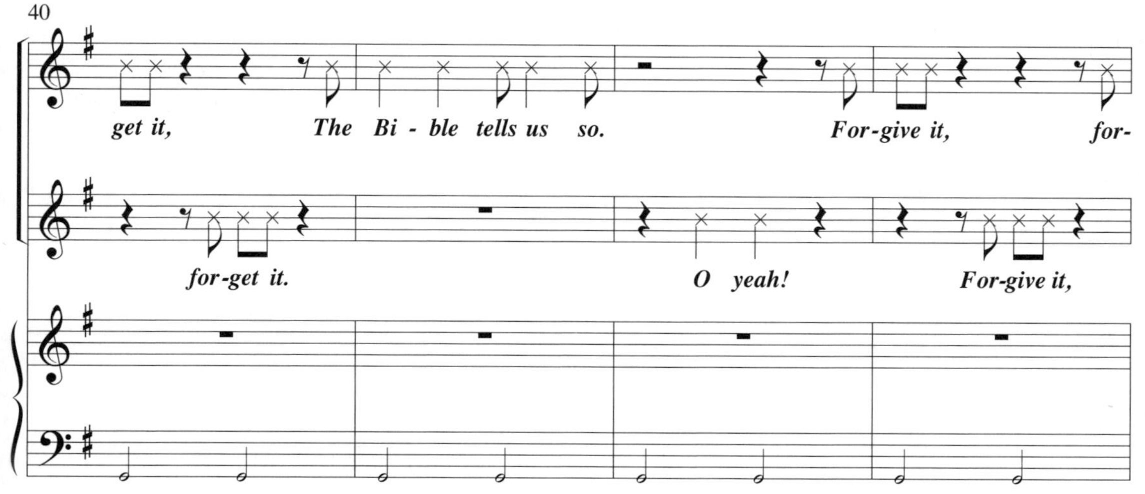

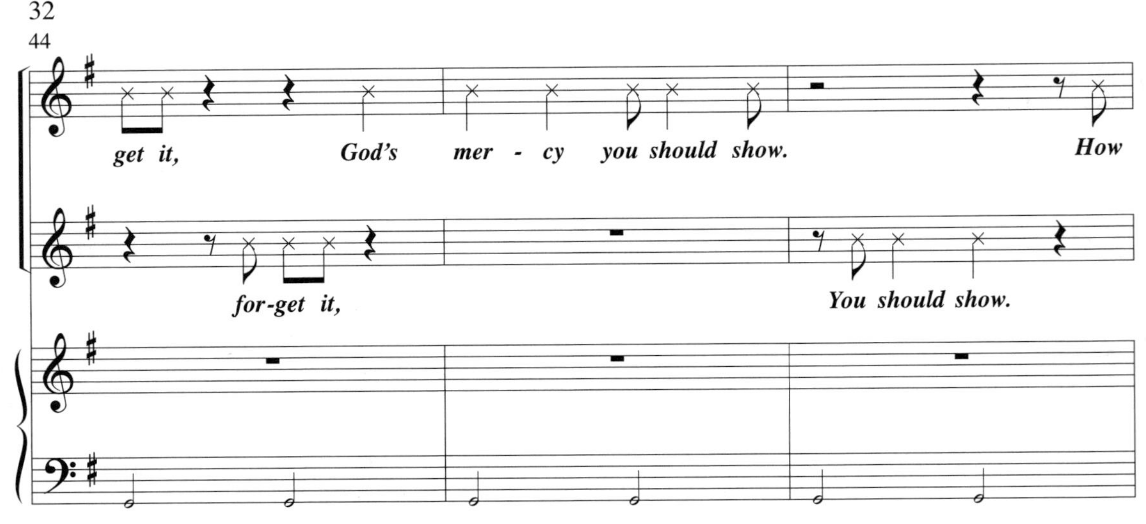
44
get it, God's mer - cy you should show. How
for-get it, You should show.

47
man - y times should we for-give these wrongs that come each day?

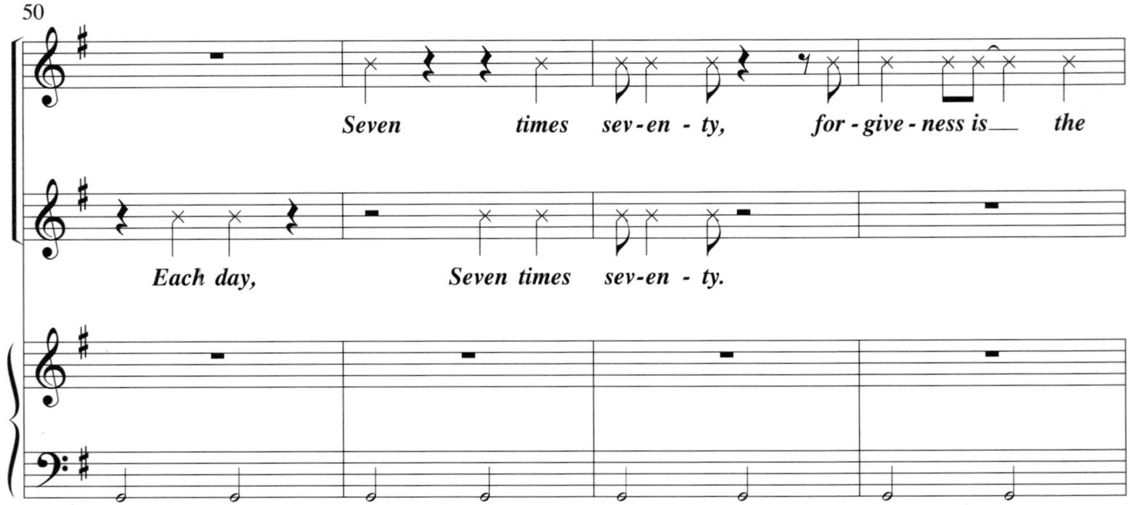
50
Seven times sev-en - ty, for - give - ness is the
Each day, Seven times sev-en - ty.

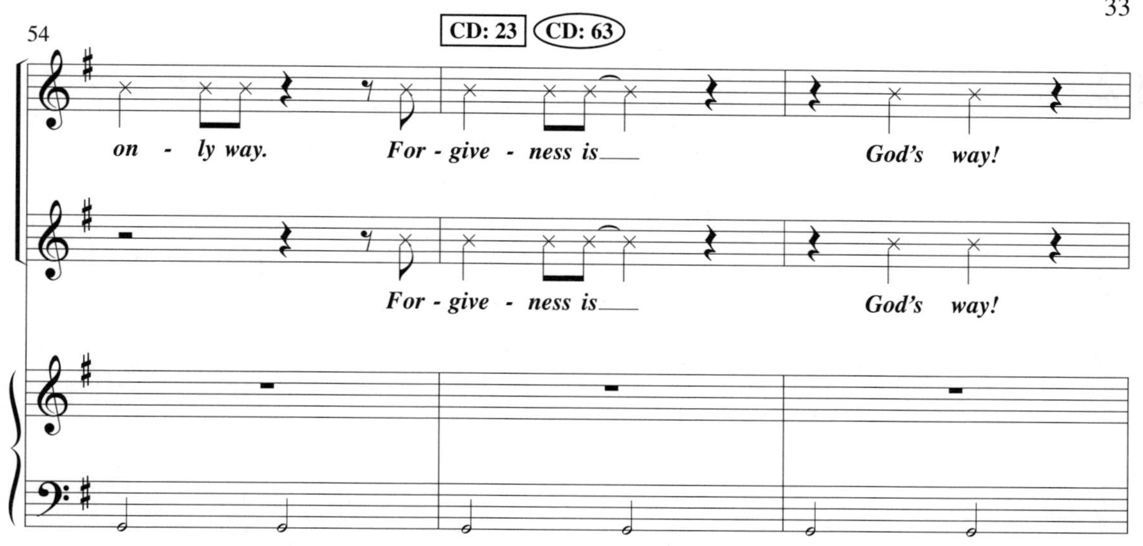
54
CD: 23
CD: 63
on - ly way. For - give - ness is God's way!
For - give - ness is God's way!

57
CHOIR
f
You got-ta for - give and for-get,
G
D♭
E♭
A♭
D♭
f

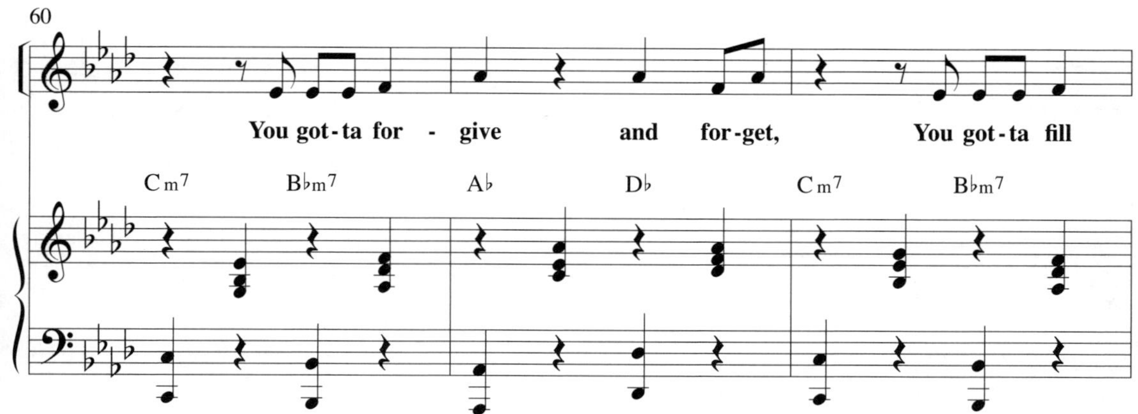
60
You got-ta for - give and for-get, You got-ta fill
Cm7
B♭m7
A♭
D♭
Cm7
B♭m7

63

up your heart with heav'n - ly joy and

A♭ F$^{\sharp 9}_{7}$

65

Je - sus' hap - pi - ness. So when some -

B♭9 Cm7 D♭6 B♭7/D E♭

8vb

67

one has done you wrong, Just give it to Je - sus in a song.

A♭ C7 D♭

70

In or-der to live, you got-ta for - give and for-get.

B♭7 B♭m7 E♭7sus

SCENE 5

ASHLEY: It wasn't easy for me to forgive Shelli. She had really hurt me. But then I realized I had to forgive her because Jesus had forgiven me. When Jesus died on the cross, He forgave my sins. And when we accept His forgiveness, He tells us He forgets our sin and puts it as far as the east is from the west. My custom-built heart needed a serious tune up. Jesus helped me to forgive Shelli and finally put it all behind me. *(Music begins)* He's the one who gives me the power to stay strong in the race of life. And now I have a million reasons to praise Him with all my heart and with everything I am!

Praise My King

Words and Music by
CARTER ROBERTSON
and BARNY ROBERTSON
Arr. by Barny Robertson

ev - 'ry - thing I am.
I'm gon - na
D♭
E♭
B♭m7
N.C.

11
lift my voice! (Lift my voice!) I'm gon - na lift my voice, I
B♭m7
C m7
B♭m7

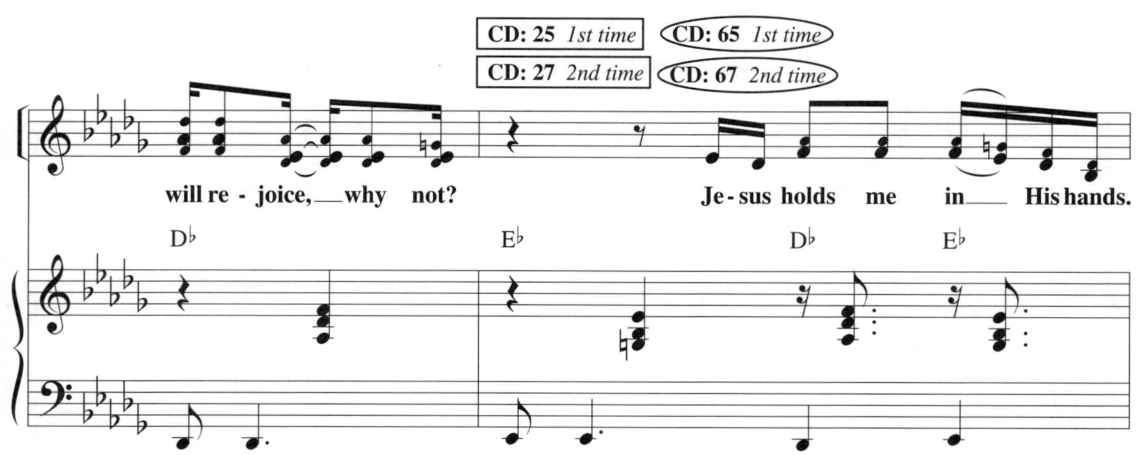
CD: 25 1st time
CD: 27 2nd time
CD: 65 1st time
CD: 67 2nd time
will re - joice, why not?
Je - sus holds me in His hands.
D♭
E♭
D♭
E♭

14

1. He had a plan before the world began, He gave His life for everyone. A-

2. He set me free from my imprisoned soul, He broke the chains of the enemy's lies. Now for the

B♭m7 E♭7 E♭/G

B♭m7 D♭ E♭7 E♭/G B♭m7 D♭

CD: 26 *1st time* CD: 66 *1st time*

CD: 28 *2nd time* CD: 68 *2nd time*

17

maz - ing grace, won - drous love, He is the might-y, might-y Lord, God's

first time in my life I am whole, If I don't sing to Him the rocks will

E♭7 E♭/G B♭m7 D♭ Cm7 E♭

19
(to pg. 36, meas. 7)
on - ly Son.
I'm gon - na praise my King!
cry out!
Fsus
F
(to pg. 36, meas. 7)
B♭m7

Sing cues both times
(Praise my King!) I'm gon-na praise my King, give Him ev - 'ry - thing I got,
Cm7
B♭m7
D♭

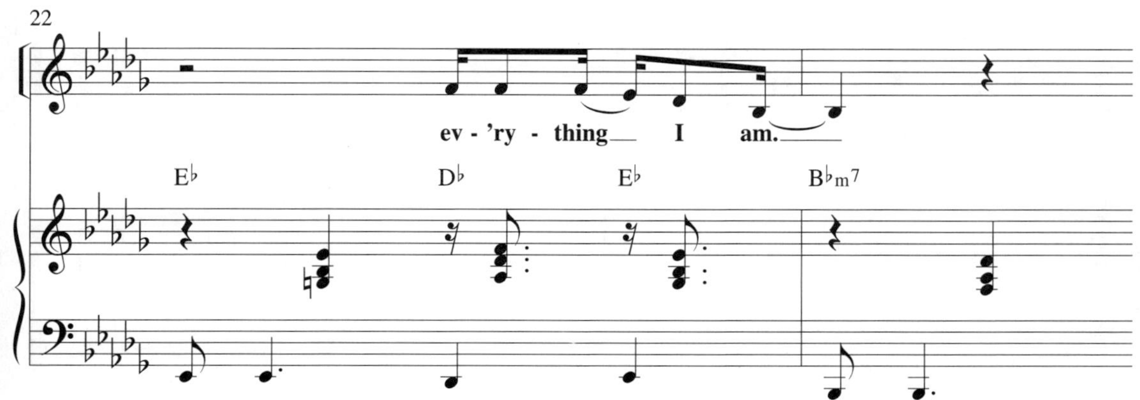
22
ev - 'ry - thing I am.
E♭
D♭
E♭
B♭m7

I'm gon-na lift my voice! (Lift my voice!) I'm gon-na
N.C.
B♭m7
Cm7

CD: 29 1st time
CD: 69 1st time
CD: 30 2nd time
CD: 70 2nd time
25
lift my voice, I will re - joice, why not? Je-sus
B♭m7
D♭
E♭

(to pg. 39, meas. 20)
f
holds me in His hands. I'm gon-na
D♭
E♭
B♭m7
N.C.
f

28
praise my King! (Praise my King!) I'm gon - na praise my King!
B♭m7
C m7
D♭M7

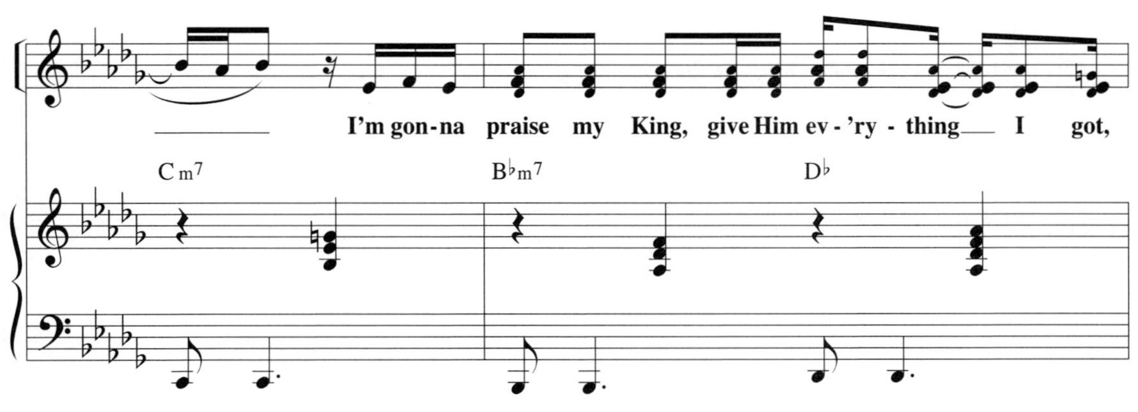
I'm gon-na praise my King, give Him ev - 'ry - thing I got,
C m7
B♭m7
D♭

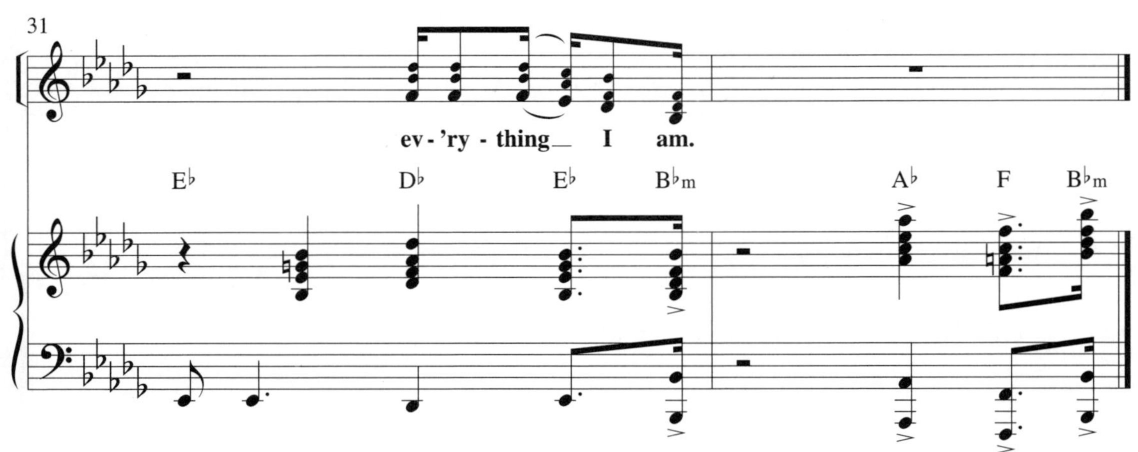
31
ev - 'ry - thing I am.
E♭
D♭
E♭
B♭m
A♭
F
B♭m

SCENE 6

*(*JULIE, JIMMY, *and* ASHLEY *stand at microphones)*

JULIE *(to* JIMMY*)*: It looks to me like you've got a custom-built heart!

JIMMY: You know it!

JULIE: Sorry about the glitter on your racecar. Forgive me?

JIMMY: I forgive you.

ASHLEY: Between you and me, I'd say we've got forgiveness covered.

JULIE: So now we have everything it takes to race well?

JIMMY: Let me check. *(Looking at his clipboard)*

ASHLEY: We've got love.

JIMMY: Check. *(Uses a pen to check each item off)*

JULIE: Prayer.

JIMMY: Check.

ASHLEY: Forgiveness.

JIMMY: Check.

JULIE: Praise.

JIMMY: Check. *(Looking at his clipboard)* Hmmm. We're still missing something.

ASHLEY: Really?

JULIE: What else does it take?

ALL KIDS *(including Choir)*: It takes Action!

Action

Words and Music by
CARTER ROBERTSON
and BARNY ROBERTSON
Arr. by Barny Robertson

13
I'm step - pin' out, gon - na be a light, His
D/F♯
D/G
15
love has set me free!
I'm turn - in' my back
C2
D/C
A sus
D
18
on the old life, In Christ I've got a new life.
D
C2
D
CD: 32 1st time
CD: 72 1st time
CD: 34 2nd time
CD: 74 2nd time
21
I'm step - pin' out, gon - na be a light, His
D/F♯
D/G

23
love has set me free! It takes ac - tion!
C2 A sus D N.C. D
26
Walk - in' a new walk. Ac - tion!
Em7 D/F♯
28
Talk - in' a new talk. Ac - tion!
G2 D/A
30
Think - in' new thoughts, His love has set me free!
G2/B C2 D/C

32
It takes ac - tion!
Walk-in' a new walk.
D
Em7
CD: 35 2nd time
CD: 75 2nd time
35
Ac - tion!
Talk-in' a new talk.
Ac - tion!
D/F♯
G2
D/A
38
Think - in' new thoughts, His love has set me free!
G2/B
C2
D/C
D
CD: 33
CD: 73
40
1
Bm
D

43
(to pg. 43, meas. 9)
2
It takes
C
A sus
D
A sus
D
A sus
46
ac - tion!
His love has set me–
D
E m7
48
Ac - tion!
His love has set me–
D/F♯
G 2
50
cresc.
Ac - tion!
His love has set me free!
ff
D/A
C
D
cresc.
ff

SCENE 7

(The same two ANNOUNCERS *from the first scene sit in their same places behind the table.)*

ANNOUNCER 1: We've definitely seen some "Action" today, *(name of* ANNOUNCER 2*)*.

ANNOUNCER 2: That's right *(name of* ANNOUNCER 1*)*. And it's not over yet!

ANNOUNCER 1: With just a few more laps to go, these custom-built hearts have been racing for their lives.

ANNOUNCER 2: That's the truth! But then, what do you expect when they're filled up, prayed up, and headed the right way?

ANNOUNCER 1: I expect "High Performance" from these drivers right up to the end.

ANNOUNCER 2: And the end is in sight! The crowd goes wild! *(Kids all cheer)*

ANNOUNCER 1: Now it's all about that finish line!

ANNOUNCER 2: And this isn't the finish line of just any race.

ANNOUNCER 1: No, ladies and gentlemen, this is . . .

ALL KIDS *(including Choir)*: "The Race of Your Life!"

(After the song, you can use one of the songs for bow music and/or have the pastor come up for final words.)

High Performance Mind
(Fill It Up!)

Words and Music by
CARTER ROBERTSON
and BARNY ROBERTSON
Arr. by Barny Robertson

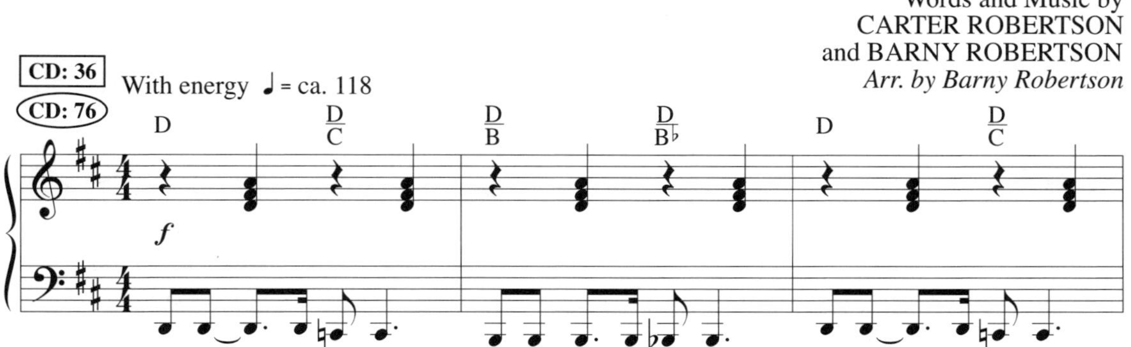

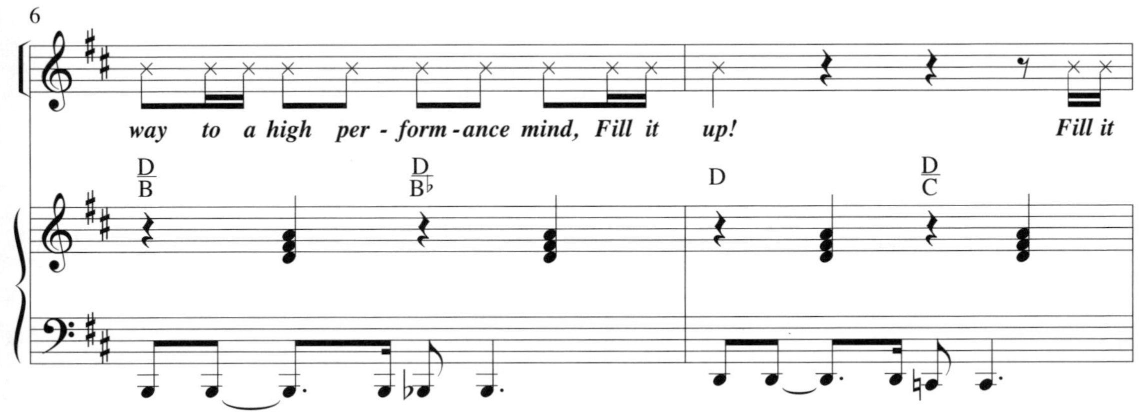

8

up! Trans - formed by the truth,

D/B D/B♭ D D/C

10

let your life be liv - ing proof, Live it out! Live it

D/B D/B♭ D D/C

12

out! **Here are the most im - port - ant com -**

D/B D/B♭ A (no3)

CD: 37 *1st time* CD: 77 *1st time*

CD: 39 *2nd time* CD: 79 *2nd time*

14

mand - ments of all. Let's start to be smart and

B♭(no3)/A C(no3)/A

16
Both times: GROUP 1
an - swer Je - sus' call.
Love the
2nd time only: GROUP 2
Love the
A sus
18
Lord your God, with all your heart, with all your soul, your strength and mind. That's
Lord your God, with all your soul, your strength and mind. That's
D
G
C
A sus
20
one! That's num - ber one!
one! That's num - ber one!
D
G
C
A sus

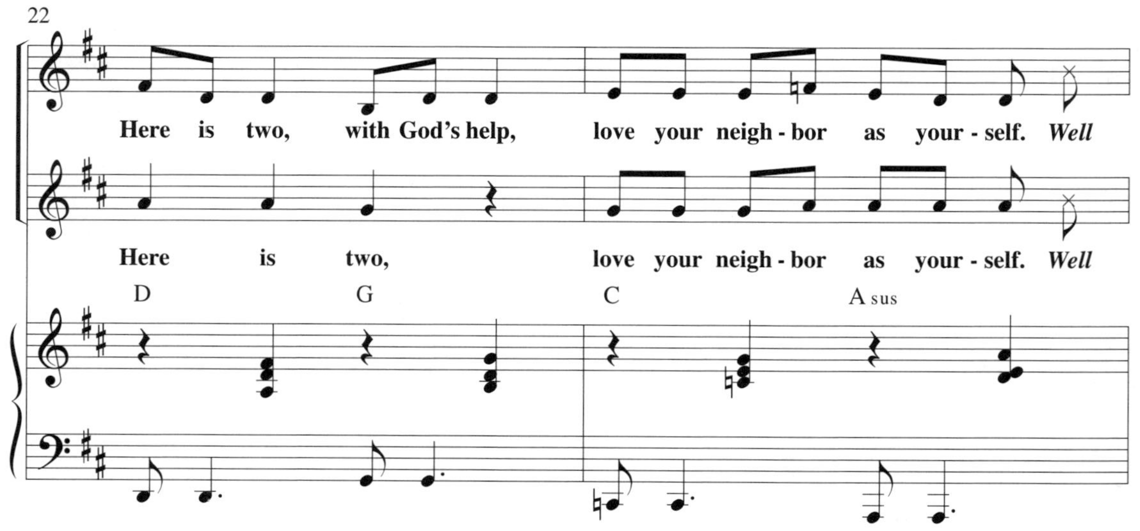
22
Here is two, with God's help, love your neigh - bor as your - self. *Well*
Here is two, love your neigh - bor as your - self. *Well*
D
G
C
A sus

24
done! *You did it! Well done!* Love the
done! *You did it! Well done!* Love the
D
G
C
A sus

26
Lord your God, with all your heart, with all your soul, your strength and mind. *That's*
Lord your God, with all your soul, your strength and mind. *That's*
D
G
C
A sus

28
one! That's num-ber one! Here is two, with God's help,
one! That's num-ber one! Here is two,
D G C A sus D G
31
CD: 40 2nd time
CD: 80 2nd time
love your neigh-bor as your-self. Well done! You did it! Well
love your neigh-bor as your-self. Well done! You did it! Well
C A sus D G
33
1 CD: 38 CD: 78
(to pg. 49, meas. 5)
done!
done!
1
(to pg. 49, meas. 5)
C A sus D D/C D/B D/B♭

36
2
ALL
In God's Word you can find the way to a high per - form - ance mind, Fill it
D
D/C
D/B
D/B♭
38
up! Fill it up!
D
D/C
D/B
D/B♭
40
Trans - formed by the truth, let your life be liv - ing proof, Live it
D
D/C
D/B
D/B♭
42
out! Live it out!
D
8vb

PRODUCTION NOTES

by Heidi Petak

Revved Up and Ready to Go! is a musical for kids involving speaking roles for 5 boys and 5 girls but you'll find some of the roles are adjustable to your needs. There are also a couple of non-speaking roles in the cast.

CAST

ANNOUNCER 1 - Male, enthusiastic, good enunciation, announces the beginning and end of the race. Wears a button-up shirt, tie, and headphones.

ANNOUNCER 2 - Female, enthusiastic, good enunciation, announces the beginning and end of the race. Wears a nice shirt and headphones.

JULIE - Little sister of JIMMY, precocious but with a positive attitude. Wears casual clothing.

JIMMY - Big brother of JULIE, has less of a positive attitude than his sister, must be able to snap his fingers. Wears casual clothing.

HAROLD - Husband of HENRIETTA, stubborn, older man. Wears adult clothing and glasses.

HENRIETTA - Wife of HAROLD, confused, older woman. Wears adult clothing and glasses.

MIKE - Authoritative, persuasive. Wears a trench coat and sunglasses.

CLICK - Brother of TICK, radio personality, expert on cars. Wears an auto mechanic jumpsuit.

TICK - Sister of CLICK, radio personality, expert on cars. Wears an auto mechanic jumpsuit.

ASHLEY - Frustrated caller to CLICK and TICK'S radio show, sensitive, spiritual and emotional. Wears casual clothing.

NON-SPEAKING ROLES: RACER 1 and RACER 2 *(these two kids race for a candy bar in Scene 1)* and optional a girl to play SHELLI when ASHLEY pantomimes calling her.

PROPS

Scene 1: 1 table, 2 chairs, 2 pairs of headphones, 2 table mics

Scene 2: Glitter-painted racecar for Jimmy

Scene 3: 4 chairs, map for Henrietta

Scene 4: 1 table, 2 chairs, 2 pairs of headphones, 2 table mics, cell phone for Ashley

Scene 6: Pen and clipboard for Jimmy

Scene 7: 1 table, 2 chairs, 2 pairs of headphones, 2 table mics

SET DESIGN

Since car racing is the theme of this musical, utilize the primary colors of NASCAR in your set: yellow, red, purple, blue, green. Position 8-10 tall, primary colored flags across the right, left, and back edges of the stage. Display a primary-colored banner above the choir that reads, "Revved Up and Ready to Go!"

Instead of using choir risers, consider using stacks of tires with sheets of plywood laid across them as "platforms" for groups of kids to stand on. Or, you could use choir risers for the kids and still have a few stacks of tires placed on the edges of the stage for visual interest.

As with the set for any musical, you may choose to be as minimal or as extravagant as you would like in your design. For small churches working in a small space, consider keeping your set minimal. For large churches working in a large space, you may need to obtain larger banners, flags, and tires to provide your entire audience with a visual experience.

COSTUMES

See character notes for costumes for speaking roles. Kids in the choir wear different primary colored, plain t-shirts and different colored ball caps on backwards. You can also order t-shirts with the musical logo from:

Personalized Gift and Apparel	Tom Roland, Owner (888) 898 6172
Website: www.pg4u.com	Email: info@pg4u.com

MOVEMENTS

Movement ideas for the songs in this musical are found on the Lillenas website on the *Revved Up and Ready to Go!* product page. Go to www.lillenas.com.